pebbles of imagination

NERIYA M VENKAT

INDIA • SINGAPORE • MALAYSIA

ISBN 979-8-89233-759-5

Dedication

I would like to dedicate my book to my parents. They are my true heroes! My little brother has supported me on this incredible journey, especially when I got writers block. I hope you enjoy this book.

Contents

Contents

1
Flipping in the air

When I am doing gymnastics, I feel fan-flipping-tastic! (no pun intended). Gymnastics makes me feel free. Whether I am doing beautiful cartwheels or precise back walkovers, I feel I can jump up in the sky and fly.

My favourite thing to do in gymnastics is to make my own floor routines. Whether you are a beginner gymnast or you an expert, floor routines are a mix of easy and hard movements. Making a floor routine consists of remembering the moves, having perfect aim and balance and being graceful.

Being graceful involves four steps:

- Stretch: The best way to make you sure of any minor slip-ups as well as make you graceful as a swan.
- Practice: As Bruce Lee once said, I am not scared of a man who has practiced 100 moves, I fear a man who has practised one move 100 times.

- Feedback: If you are having troubles try and see where you are wrong, ask for feedback it never hurts.
- Improvement: Look yourself in the mirror so you exactly know where you can come in with another move to make it look better.

Never hold back yourself if you have a talent. Show your talent. Do not be afraid to be you. There may be criticisms, but you just keep on going. You are amazing, you got this.

2
Hope

Anyone who asks what hope is or how to explain hope is either going to get short answer or a mixed answer which may not be the best to understand.

So, I am going to explain hope in a way that everyone can understand. An explanation of hope isn't just a bunch of words or synonyms of hope put together.

Hope is not just a word. Hope is a feeling that we all get but currently in this age it's scarce. Hope does not happen on its own. It takes its own time. When there is hatred, negative and toxic situations, this becomes a warning sign for hope not to visit us.

Whereas empathy, kindness and good spirits become a mall for hope. Hope comes in and once they are done with their work, they leave waiting for the reality to kick in.

There is an opposite of hope. But that does not exist. So, you might be asking why? Although many people believe that the opposite of hope is synonyms of hopeless such as despair, but there is no such thing in reality.

As we evolved our human brains grew into mindsets. Everything one wants may not always happen all the time. It is completely random. So many stopped behaving well because one did not get what one wanted.

But a lucky few on this big blue beautiful earth still believe in the truth about hope which serves their mindset right. Mindsets change over time and its natural. But we need to keep remembering to stay positive and the state of the mindset matters.

3
En pointe

There are two perspectives of ballet. One perspective sees ballet as waste of time. The other sees how hard it is to go up en pointe. It is hard.

I think the most mesmerizing thing about ballet is its pointes. The pointes, they are a hit and run situation. When you go up on pointe, all the stress, tension, and hardworking sweat stays where it is.

When I first tried pointe, I was on Nike, and I was constantly falling forward and backward. After that, I kept doing it repeatedly until I could do a full 360.

I'm not that good at pointe, but seeing that I am in the third level, and usually you start pointe at the fifth, gave me a boost in confidence. Pointe shoes are also, especially important. Every dancer has their own unique shoe.

Pointe shoes have a triangle like front and ribbons that wind up your leg. They have a triangle like base because it's simply easier. Have you ever tried doing pointe on Crocs? You would find that it is simply easier. From the support and rubber material, it's quite easy to go up on your toes. You can try it out today!

The perfect pointe shoes don't have any rubber, but are tight and flexible, so that it's easier to go up with them. If you have had ballet training before, you would know that if you go up on pointe too much, it hurts. The pain will get concentrated on your tippy toes and all the joints and bones crack.

I know it all sounds anticipating doing something wonderful like this, but I beg of you to not try this at home, as it needs expert training. So, next time you see someone do ballet and go up en pointe, try not to be jealous!

4
Ikigai

Have you ever heard of ikigai? It's a Japanese concept, "your purpose in life". But what does that even mean?

Celebrities in the world grew up knowing what their purpose in life was. But how do we find it? It's more of a DIY thing. Only you can find your purpose in life. Many people have gone head over heels for this kind of stuff. But the authentic way to find yourself is to be you. But how do we do that?

Let us say that I like to play the piano. I keep practising it until I am so good, that I enter the nationals. I win the gold and go on to become a world-famous composer and pianist. Now, the very first thing to do is to find out at what you are good at.

Take your interests and push yourself to do what you do best. And no, watching TV for 35 hours straight that does not count! But there can be a workaround.

YouTubers get a lot of money from making content, so maybe try uploading videos that you are sure will get a LOT of views.

But first things first, do not give up. The best way to have this is a mindset to remind yourself that you won't get success instantly. But that does not mean you have to stop trying. Eventually, you will get more subscribers and views and you will skyrocket.

The best way to motivate yourself is to keep trying. Go on and on and do not ever stop. Because the more you keep trying, the less you will become a lazy person and you will have everything that you ever wanted.

5

Sustainability

Do you know what sustainability means? Sustainability is where all initiatives respect and appreciate nature and secure it for future generations. For example: tourist travels are not earth-friendly and tourist places such as hotels and outdoor cafés use too much plastic and packaging, but what can we do?

Earth is our one and only world, so if we take too much of an advantage, then there is no other option than for us to go partially extinct. And we do not want that.

Children have dreams. They run with their ideas and without children, this world practically go poof! My point here is kids' ideas can help the earth.

Kids, if you ever see someone so ambitious to create their own brand or business, tell them try to respect the environment and the culture of the local people. Money is not the only thing that is important. If humans went extinct money would be just a piece of paper and have no value.

By just planting a few trees, we are not only making the earth greener, but we are also helping ourselves. The more trees we plant, the more oxygen we get, and it's all good for the planet. If you are going to make something, at least make it sustainable that appreciates nature. It helps everyone. Save the planet. It is the only one with pizza in it :)

6
Bullying

At least every other kid has experienced bullying, but not in ways the way we know best. It could just be normal bullying, where they just call you names.

Name calling by far is the most popular type of bullying. Every school has those people who call others by names, like "dumb," "idiotic" and so on. The most common way to bully someone is fight against gender. As kids we think that their own gender is superior to the other. They start by saying mean stuff towards the other gender and then eventually saying sentences like, "nobody likes you, you are so dumb, just shut up."

In reality the best way to tackle the beginning stage of bullying is to be quiet. If you tell an adult that some one is saying mean things to you, then they are going to make it public, and the person will be even more mad with you and bully you more. So, the best way to deal with the beginning stage is to be quiet. But, if it develops into a repeated pattern, leads to physical harm, then it's time to yell at the top of your lungs. The adults know what to do and can manage it more than you can.

It is always good to spread awareness on bullying, especially when you cannot handle it anymore. It feels like you can handle it on your own, but you really can't. In many ways, it is extremely harmful for you to hold on to and hide something that happened to you. I know it feels scary. To be pushed around by others and just lose control for a few seconds. If you act everything is fine, and don't mind at all then you can become mentally ill, and it can cause lots of problems. Speaking up is the best that you can do.

7
How not be bored

Have not we all been bored before? It is the saddest thing ever. Now, here are a couple of things that you should do if you get bored easily.

- Do not compel yourself to read. This just makes things so much more boring, especially if you are forced to. Also, remember that you cannot just stare at a page full of boring words, that just takes away all the fun.
- Do not sit still. Move around, learn to do a cartwheel, or something that you have any interest in. Except for the things where you need stuff to help you achieve the goal. How may you ask? Well, a piano for example. You cannot buy one, but you also want to play it. So, try avoiding those interests that cost money. Do something else like jumping around like a bean and create some games. Get your toys and play around with them.
- Find ways to be creative, like create your own board game. Craft something, like a chatterbox or

do some origami. Challenge yourself to things that you wouldn't normally do, step outside of your comfort zone.

My most favourite thing to go with is just cooking. I like to turn on my cooking fire, and just focus on that for a while. Cooking is impressive. My favourite thing to do, is to toast bread, cut cheese into rectangles, put butter on the toast, lay the cheese slices and add chocolate buttons. So, as I was saying, do anything that interests you, and try out new things. It never hurts.

8
Creative writing

Haven't we all wondered, "is it possible to write a majestic poem, or a really expressive story?" Well, I am here to help you on this creative journey. I will get you going to finish your goal and achieve more than what you wished for! So, let us go by, step by step.

- Get a notebook and a pen. Or a pencil. Whatever works best for you. I prefer using a pen, because it writes better than a pencil, in which generally the lead breaks. You can also use a sheet of paper or a computer instead of a notebook. But if you are using paper, get a file or a binder and dedicate it to your writing, and if it becomes a wonderful habit, then you will have something glorious to look back on.
- Start thinking of things that interest you. For me, its mythology. I love to write things about the other side of the galaxy, where unicorns riding on sharks wearing a tutu gliding through a rainbow. For stories let your mind go wild, while for poems

express them in ways that you would try. Poems can be rhyming. But it does not have to have a good timing! Ha-ha! You see what I just did there? That is a case of rhyming words. You can also use different synonyms. Like this: I love clouds, that's why I save my data in the cloud.

- Keep the idea straight. For me and probably a million other people out there are having a problem with ideas. You see, I love to write stories, when I do, a few minutes later, I get another idea for a story, I just go along with that, so it's VERY important to stay focused only on your main ideas. If you suffer from this already, then just jot down your thoughts, collect them a million times. So, anyone can write.

9
Little imperfections

In a world based on the look of everything, people pleasers come and go. Even the small little things people care about, like being not ugly, not too fat, not have horrible teeth, not have too many pimples, not have imperfect skin and so on.

All of this affects us in ways that we cannot think of, and it throws us off track. The best way to deal with this is to listen to yourself. You don't have to be perfect. Because everyone is unique in their own way. Don't care about what others say. They are talking rubbish when they say that you must be perfect. You don't have to be.

Our evolution is linked to judging everything by looks. Does anyone know about human zoos? No? Well then, I am here to explain to you exactly what that is. Human zoos are where people (mostly coloured or non-white) were thrown into cages where eventually they would be fed with some mushy gruel in a bowl.

People from all around the world would come to see people locked up in cages, sometimes naked as well. This caused a major stir in those days functioning and it wasn't right. It's quite absurd that people know how this way of living was wrong, but they said nothing.

This past is linked because although as humans we made grave mistake, we have changed our ways, and have become more empathetic. People have started to be more understanding of others and how they are treated.

If you are the one who feels something, SHOUT IT OUT! It doesn't matter if anyone disagrees with you, just follow your own instincts, and say what you want to. Standing up for what is yours isn't wrong.

10

Maybe, or maybe not

We live in a world where the unknown is common. There are so many things that us humans don't know, and I'm referring this to humans as there may be other life forms, but since our technology isn't as advanced as other life forms that may be out there, we don't really know for sure.

My best fantasy is that what if mermaids were real? Imagine that they lived under water and swam freely in the ocean? Imagine that corona virus never happened. We all lived in a giant ocean city. I was going to a shop, and checked out the glimmering sea tails, and bought a beautiful one, where it had a gradient of blue and pink, with shiny scales and sequins. And we also had witches, two of them, one good and one bad. They both help their costumers, but the bad one helps with more darker problems... anyway!

This town is in the Pacific, and their rulers are a group that stays deep, deep down in the darkest trench, the Mariana Trench, also known as the challenger of the deep. They stay there, and come up every once and awhile, riding giant Megalodons. This world is my dream.

I want to ride with dolphins and go splash into the waves. This might all seem pretty and kept, but there is one thing that is holding them back. For those who don't know, every pleasantry has its secrets. And for the poor citizens of this world, they live in the fear of the deep dark in the Mariana Trench.

Although the rulers stay there, they are mind controlled. They are trying to escape, but it's no use. Ever since they went down into that trench, they have been trapped, and forced to do the bidding of a giant sea monster, but that's a story for another time.

11
Modern Ghosts

Most of us think that ghosts aren't real. What if ghosts were real and all the dead turned into sprits and are now cursed on this big blue sphere which we call home?

I mean, it is possible. Just imagine ghosts going out into this world and learning new stuff every day. The dead souls could be wandering in an Apple store, and they should be either scratching their heads or finally getting the hang of using an iPhone. I mean, how crazy would that be!

But here is where it gets interesting. Let's say, that I am a ghost, and I want to go and eat somewhere. Yes, did you know that ghosts and spirits can eat?

There is a cafe nearby. I walk into the cafe and look at the menu. Croissants, sugar glazed donuts, cakes, cookies, tea, coffee and hot chocolate with some marshmallows.

I decide to order the cookies. To place an order, I am going to possess an adult. Luckily for me, I see one. I fly towards that human and go inside its body. Then, once I eat the cookies I leave the body. See, how easy that is.

12
Android vs Apple

We have all heard about which device is better, Android or Apple? I am going to list down top five things to make the case.

- Phone appearance: for this round, we will have to give it to Apple. I mean Android has its looks, but it does not match with Apple. The looks of Apple are filled with aesthetic and just good looking overall.
- Which one works better: Generally, IOS devices are faster and smoother than the Android.
- How about taking photos: In this round Android has won. Android phone that I have used had an option of pausing the video, so it makes the video cuts without any hard editing work.
- Which one costs less: Of course, Android. Apple iPhones can cost a fortune and dent your pocket.
- Which is more secure: IOS devices are more secure and more private. So, Apple is slightly more protective and secure of your data.

To conclude Apple is better in many ways. Although, Android is quite good as well, technically Apple wins. So next time your parents say no to an iPhone make them a presentation about how Apple's benefits. It is far more secure and protects privacy.

13

Success

Have you ever felt like you wanted to just sit at home do nothing and watch some TV, play on gadgets and snack on pizza. Well, now, you can!

All depends on what you do. You can easily become popular and famous. And here's what you do.

Be productive. If you are student, then the first thing you need to do is study well. I know it seems like a lot to do but being productive is a good start.

Be committed. No matter what anyone says to you, you shouldn't give up. If someone push you down, you get back up again. But if you are having trouble bouncing back then here are few things you need to know.

Build connections. Share your ideas with anyone and go wild with it. Your idea doesn't have to be secret from the world, tell others, and just keep on going.

Have a good mindset. It's important, especially for the perseverance part. And you need to start having a mindset early on. Then only will you be used to it and continue it through your daily life.

So, in conclusion, all you need is a good mindset, be committed, build connections, and be productive. With these skills, you can do anything!

14
Manging stress

Have you ever met one of those people who think that they are being overworked in doing so many classes. Well, meet Cash. For sake of privacy, I won't reveal the gender.

Cash is an interesting person, hates TV and loves to study maths and science. Cash hopes to be a scientist when grown up.

Cash absolutely hates being asked whether Cash is free anytime of the week. Because Cash always finds an excuse to talk about all the times Cash is busy and clouded up with classes to make Cash the smartest kid in the school.

OK, here are all the reasons that Cash is just a show-off. First, not everyone cares enough to hear about your personal issues. So, why bother? Everyone feels overworked at some point in their life. The problem is people find an excuse to boast about how overworked they are. Sometimes it might be true. But that doesn't mean you have to play the victim. Also, if you are trying to get sympathy from others then just stop. OK? No one likes a sympathy beggar. So, if you are one, try to change your ways before you become sympathy addicted. When people care for you and ask you if you are feeling OK or not, that's the place where you go and spill the beans about your stress.

Now, here are some tips to deal with stress. Get a journal or a diary to write your feelings and emotions down. This is highly effective for all sorts of ages especially teens as they go through a lot of hardships through their adolescent life. Also, if you ever find yourself in any stressful situation try doing the things you love the most. It can be a hobby or an instrument or doing something that makes you happy.

15

What food to order in a French Café

Have you ever wanted to be able to go authentic French café? When you get there, you don't know what to order. Well, I'm here to help you out on that, pal. Here are the top five foods to eat at a French café.

- French café will delight you with their buttery croissants with fluffy layers tucked in.
- Macrons are a meringue filled sandwich cookie. It comes in almost any flavour like strawberry, pistachio, chocolate and is a very colourful delight.
- Pain au chocolat is a chocolatey version of the croissant with gooey chocolate oozing out when you bite.
- Profiteroles are basically cream puff filled with almost anything like cream or meringue. They burst into flavour once you bite them.

- Crepe is a French version of a pancake but thinner, add an extra dose of sweet chocolate and fruits like strawberry or banana.

So, these are some of the top foods that you can order in French café. Bon appetite!

16
School shooting

Have you ever heard about school shooting? Well, it's a serious problem. It is a sad truth it happens. It's like, I'm in a bad mood so I guess I'm just gonna go shoot people at school. OK, it is not actually like that, but you get my point, right? School shooting happens frequently in some parts of the world. Let me explain how it feels.

I listen quietly as maths teacher rambles on and on about some math, and I just decide to doodle food the entire time. The teacher notices, strides all the way to my seat and just as the teacher was to finish the sentence, a person with a gun in hand bursts through the door. Before anyone can say anything, "Bang! Bang!" I was the first one to get under the table, and the last one to leave the classroom when it all got over.

The faint sound of a gun shooting plays in my head as I hear a police car siren. I walk speechless through the bodies with blood. I walk all the way out of school and to home. My parents comforted me as much as they could. But nothing could make me forget that day. Ever.

Scary, right? The worst part, at least some kids of all ages have experienced this.

I am not proud to say that this situation has exactly gotten better. But from what we can do, I say, we can work together to fix this. We do our best to enforce laws that say, 'no guns at homes'. Even the small acts can help our children. By working together, we can save each other.

17

Trinity College music exams

This is my experience about how to take trinity grade exams for vocals.

First, don't practice too much. Because then the song will get stuck in your head. By the time you realise you will be singing it. And your friends will think you're weird.

Second, practice last minute. Because then you will know the pieces fresh in your memory. Practice for minimum 20mins every day.

Third, be confident but not too confident. If you are overconfident you mess up the timing, note and so on. So be confident on an average level.

Fourth, believe in yourself. Have faith and trust in yourself because a good mindset leads to good outcomes.

Finally, talk to your teacher about how to manage nervousness. They are professionals and will help you manage the nervousness.

In conclusion, all these tips are guaranteed to help you to excel Trinity College music exams. The best thing to do is always calm yourself to have a peace of mind, that way you have a higher probability of improving and maybe getting a distinction.

18

Ways to be thankful

Everyone has heard people saying that being thankful is better for you. But what does that mean? Let me explain.

The easiest way to be thankful is to be mindful. It means you are aware of what is happening in front of you, behind you and around you. Being mindful helps you to realise that not everything revolves around you is always nice. Let's take the Israel Gaza War, Russia Ukraine war or earthquake in Syria for example. People don't usually realise that they hold privilege. They don't have to worry about any bombs going off and they don't have to worry about rubble falling on their heads. They live the good life and for that they should be thankful for.

The next way to be thankful is to do something you enjoy. You should be thankful for the things that you love to do, because you will only get to enjoy them for a short amount of time. Life is short. Not many people live as long as average people. So be thankful for the things you enjoy and love doing.

Another way to be thankful is to succeed. If you have succeeded in succeeding, then you have one more reason to be thankful. You have what you wished for. May be money, although money is not everything it is one of the privileges in life. There is more to life than money.

These are some of the ways you get started to be thankful in everything you do. Being thankful isn't a skill. Although it is something you learn to do, it is something that is inside you. Unless you have the power and motivation, being thankful isn't going to work out at all. Anyone can be thankful only if you put your mind to it.

19
How to go on scratch

Have you ever wanted to program something? That you can edit to your hearts content? Well, here is a solution. Scratch. Before I get started, I would like you to know, Scratch is popular. But if you don't know, it's OK. I will get you to express your inner voice through Scratch. But what is Scratch?

Scratch is a child friendly programming application. There are three versions of Scratch. Scratch Ed, Scratch Jr and Scratch.

Scratch Jr is a program for kids, that you can download on almost any device. While Scratch provides unlimited access to coding, Scratch ED provides basic and easy to understand controls for children to use.

OK. Now, let's get started! To join scratch, you might need to have an email address ready if you want to continue working on scratch. Now, the first thing you do is type, "scratch," on your search bar, and up will come the website. Click on the link and you will see the home page. In the home page, click on a white button, that says, "Start

Creating," with a little star next to it. Now you're going to learn how to create.

You'll see a bright blue box on the top. You'll want to click the one that has tutorials. There are many things to do in scratch. But, first, I'm going to teach you the simplest thing I know. How to animate your name in scratch. Believe it or not, it is super easy.

Step 1. Pick a background: On the bottom right of the page, you'll see a button with a landscape and a plus. Once you click on that, it'll have five options. Upload, Random, Paint, Search, and one that takes you to the background page. This is the same for the button with the cat on it next to it. I went in order from top to bottom, so if you are following, it'll be easy! Then, you can pick any background you like. Or even create one.

Step 2. Choose your letters: You can find three versions of letter types. My favourite one is the glow type. So, you get the letters of your name, and line them up any way you want. Once you've done that, you can move onto your actions.

Step 3. Make the letters come alive: So, you name is out there. But you just want to make it come alive. Not just be a plain bold art. So, I'm going to show you how to do two things. Make your letters go rainbow and look like someone is eating them. To make them go rainbow, go to LOOKS and click on the code that says change colour effect by 25. Then, click on 25 and make it 2. The next thing you must do is get a, "when green flag clicked," block and place it above. Then, go to Control and get a forever block. Take out your change colour effect block and then put the forever block right below the green flag. Then, you can put back the change colour effect in the forever block. It's, like Lego. You're connecting the blocks to make something amazing! But, what about making someone eat the letters? Well, I'm going to show you how.

First, you are going to get a when green flag clicked block. After that, you are going to have to get a forever block. And here comes the middle. In control, get a wait one second block. Then, go to costumes. At the very bottom left of the page, there will be a Sprite button click that and just get the same alphabet. Very important thing to remember, you first need to go into costumes and get the same letter. Not on the coding homepage. Then, once you got the letter, take the eraser icon and erase some of the letter to make it look like it's been bitten. At the top, you'll see a little box and label it something good that you will remember. Then, go to looks and switch your costume to the one that has taken a bite out of it. Then, ask it to wait one second and switch it to the original. And there you have it.

All the basics you need to be a Scratch Programmer. Sure, there plenty more things to do, but these are a few that really helps you get started on you journey to being a programmer. Good luck, coders!

20

Child friendly games

Have you ever wanted to play games which are child friendly? Well, now you can! I am gonna give you some of the child friendly apps that you can download.

- Super Bear Adventure: This is a perfect offline game that you can play anywhere and anytime. With its child friendly graphics this game is perfect for all kids. With a storyline that never hits rock bottom, this game is sure to get the adventurer side of you.
- Good Pizza, Great Pizza: This game has child friendly graphics and is fun for all kids to embark on their journey of making pizza. This game is calming as well as filled with aesthetic pleasure who knew making pizza could be so fun? Well now it is! Maybe you could deliberately mess up the orders of your customers and have a little laugh.
- My Dear Farm: this game is about making a farm. The way that you would do it. This game can make your heart melt with its cuteness. Decorate your farm, your way.

Child friendly games

- Toca world is this awesome game where you make your own character and create your own house. You can cook, watch movies conducted by yourself, and even adopt so many pets that you don't have space to sleep.
- Do you have a sibling, but just on device? Or you have multiple siblings but just one device? Then download 2 player games. This app allows loads of games like chess, mini golf, and other ones which you haven't heard of before. Two player games also have a sequel, four player games. The best part about this game is that you don't have to go online and meet with other random players, you can play on the same device.

These games are perfect for everyone, and I hope you all enjoy gaming.

21
Card games

We all love playing with board games. It keeps us happy and entertained. But what about the new and improved games that don't have shout-outs? Here are some of the card games, I recommend.

- Taco, Cat, Goat, Cheese Pizza: This game is fun or everyone, as you can have up to two-eight people playing with you. With their cute minimalistic artwork, the game can have you in a coma. This game is perfect for those late-night game people, as well as just for playing. This is a perfect matching cards game.
- Guess Who card game: So, for all of you who are wondering why I picked the card game was because the board game isn't much portable, while this card game is perfect for an airplane ride or a road trip. The graphics and the images are way better, and this one is a personal favourite. Guess your opponent's card to claim championship.

- Guess in 10: This game is also available in App store. This game is where you guess something in 10 questions. This game comes in many options, like the animal kingdom, cities etc. This game is for the whole family.

All these card games are family-friendly, and perfect when you're feeling down.

22
Terrorism

Recently I read a book called, "Fight back, by A.M. Dassu". This book talks about people who are discriminated based on their religious belief. This book looks like any ordinary book from a bookstore or library. But the content is different.

Aaliyah, the main character talks about how people are slowly but surely ganging up against her and family and all Muslims in the country. People wanted to ban Muslims because they thought that terrorism and following Islam was connected. They felt like they were the outcasts. They didn't belong on this earth.

No one should have to suffer like this again. Let's stand together to fight back against discrimination.

Muslims in some parts of the world experience what Aaliyah mentions in the book. People are discriminating Muslims and treating them unfairly. They are also quite close to being kicked out of the country. What I talk about is real and not fiction and it is happening right now.

So many people are undergoing this discrimination and have no resources to help them to fight back. They are alone. But here comes the truth. Their thoughts are made to think they are going to suffer alone. But think about it this way. Almost 50% of the world experience discrimination or experiencing discrimination. What if they came together. What if they fought back. What if they stood together. Anything can become successful as long as you have teamwork. Coming together in hardships is the best thing to do. Because it helps in many ways. It helps us fight back.

Coming together is important because although you can be independent and strong but cannot do it alone. You need friends. You need supporters. You need teamwork. These are the gateways for overcoming discrimination.

23

Games you should have on a switch

Everyone has heard of the Nintendo Switch, and yes, everyone wants one, but what games are the ones that are worth it? What games makes a Nintendo Switch worth the experience? Well, I'm here to share about my favourite games on my favourite Nintendo Switch.

- Super Smash Bros: This game is perfect for those siblings out there who need to prove to each other who is better. When you have siblings, you can battle against each other and have fun unlocking new characters. This game is a personal favourite, I loved the graphics, and I had fun playing.
- Just dance 2022: This is the newly updated version, which includes better music, more songs, and good graphics. The updated version includes more actions and better dances, it also has this option which shows you how much calories, you've lost due to the dancing.

- Animal Crossing: This game is a killer, and at the top of the charts for me. This game offers peaceful playing and game money to buy your desires. This game is my favourite because you can customise it your way and have fun with it.

Nintendo games are made to give the pleasure you seek, and these are some party games that will never go out of style. So, keep playing gamers.

24

What are the best ways to ace a good score on a test?

We all have the dream of acing a test and getting full marks in the subject you don't really like, but the real question is, how do other people get better marks than ourselves? Is it because they study hard? Is it because they are just simply good at it? Well, if anything, acing a test is easy, if you follow these simple steps to success. All the better for you!

Use the internet: If you don't understand a specific topic, then the best thing to do is use the internet. With a wide variety of sources, you will be hopefully able to search your topic up and learn more about it. It will break it down for you, in ways that you may not always have thought of.

Don't waste time: Focus on modules that you hadn't before. You will only have higher chances of acing and be able to show a good result if you have given your best. Having a good motivational mindset only brings you forward, when you get distracted easily.

Revise: This helps in ways that you should be able to remember the topics that you are currently struggling to keep check in your brain. My method is to just write it down. This should help in many ways as the more you write, the more it stays in your brain.

These are only three of the many ways that you will be able to ace good marks but try using these for now. As, these are the best to use. So, I suggest no procrastinating at any circumstance. Stay resilient and stay strong!

25

The spy in the room

In the age of modern technology (which is now) many tech companies they have a secret that they have been hiding from you. Their secret is ... they are listening to you. Let me explain.

One day I was looking for videos on how to sing well. After watching three in a row, I clicked on new one. But before the video had loaded completely, I had to watch an ad. The ad was about how you could become better at singing if you logged onto this website, you'll be able to sing wonderfully.

What are the odds? I was watching videos and a completely related ad pops up and wants me desperately to click on it. This is just one of the many scenarios that have happened due to someone inventing the internet. They are listening! They are watching!

You could be on a call with your best friend with some confidential information and the phone and the app could be listening to whatever your secrets are.

To make a through point here, I'm not against technology. Heck, I use it every day! I'm just saying, be careful. Because you never know what is going on in this modern-day world. The best way to prevent this is to enable privacy settings. This helps you know what is enabled on your phone in any way links you to the internet, and you get to disable it as you wish. Good luck with the internet my friends and be safe users.

26
How cubing teaches you a lesson

I know my brother recently started cubing, and it has changed him completely. Instead of coming home to watch TV and laze around the couch and eat chips, he comes home every day to his cube and starts to scramble it up and in minutes will it be solved.

Life is like a rubix cube. When solving a rubix cube, you are going to have a lot of ups and downs. You won't be the most awesome person when it comes to the rubix cube at first. You are bound to make many mistakes on your first solve. You will take long to get your first solve done. Like that, life is similar.

In life, you might not be able to lead a great life. You will not be happy all the time. You will not be sad all the time. You will not always get the things you want. You know what's awesome about hitting rock bottom? There's only one way to go. Up!

There are no mistakes in life, only lessons. This means that when you make mistakes, those are lessons because you learn not to do them again. When there is only one way left to go, you make the most of it. You try and fail, try and fail, try and fail. Only then will you succeed.

Look at Thomas Edison for example. He tried over 100 times to make a working lightbulb. Only then did he succeed. Cubing is like this because it teaches us a very important lesson. Never give up. Never say never.

27
Active lifestyle

We have all seen people go to the gym. We see them get jacked. The workout, a diet, and they maintain a good posture. Ahh! We all wish we had that perfect body. But it's hard to get that. So, what is the best way for us to make our body better? Well, I'm here to help!

Exercise: It is very important for you to exercise because it builds your body, from the top to the bottom. Planks, Russian twists, and push ups are a good start. It builds a good core, and your upper and lower body. If you have a yoga mat in your house, take that and start stretching. You'll be surprised to see how much of a difference there is, to just start your workout with stretching. It's incredibly good for you.

Good posture: Many people find it hard to maintain their good posture, but it plays a massive role. If you maintain a good workout routine, or at least make an effort to go to the gym every day or just stretch at home, you will be progressing. Slowly but surely will your strength increase and grow. It's all the better for you!

Diet: When most people hear the word diet, healthy food and a good balance of varieties are first to come to mind, which is good. When you have enough vegetables, or you have enough fruits, it helps you. Remember meat and pulses for protein, and eggs for strength.

Maintaining an active lifestyle is more important. Follow these steps and you'll get results shortly. Keep training, kiddos!

28
Body confidence

Everyone talks about how we should be happy in our own bodies. Even if they say, you are not pretty, you have to just ignore them. But this is a way bigger problem.

Now all sizes are being shamed. If you are underweight, you are unhealthy. If you are overweight, you are still unhealthy. If you're just both, you need to lose weight, and gain it. This is a very serious problem; children are starving themselves because of the vague idea of what beauty is, that affects their health severely.

Although we are slowly but surely fixing this problem, there are others. Children are only getting influenced. Influencers influence people, ads, models and the main thing that begs my attention are mannequins.

We have all seen them in stores. Search, "mannequins with clothes," Now, let me ask you a question. Do you see thin mannequins? The answer is probably yes. But do you see oversized mannequins? Probably not. I'm not saying that it isn't being used, just that it isn't being used that often.

A lot of people, especially women and young girls are influenced to lose weight. Now, I'm not saying that having goals to lose weight is bad, it's good and I totally support it. The only problem is that some people ingest food deliberately and then throw it all up in an attempt to lose weight as well as calories. Now this isn't healthy at all.

People who work out, eat well, and have a healthy well-being are more likely to lose weight than those who eat and then vomit. For all those people who want to lose weight out there, the only way to do it is to eat healthy, workout, and maintain a positive well-being.

If they tell you that you are too thin or overweight, ignore them. If you want to change, then change. We all have to be together for this problem to resolve, and together, we can help solve this issue, faster than ever before. So those who feel insecure know that you are not alone. No one is.

29
Why Duolingo is creepy...

We all know about Duolingo and how this language learning monster got fame. In all honesty, yes, I have used Duolingo before. It's not that bad!

Duolingo released a video a while back about how they were going to enforce the "Duolingo Push,". This was simple humble reminder to finish your lesson. Duo would do things about the time left to complete the lesson, and how much work you have left. But recently, it's been creeping people out by how odd that video is. Watch it. You'll understand.

The worst thing that Duo can say is that you made him sad. But even that is creepy according to the legends. The bird is said to be ruining learner's experience. But it's only rumoured. Another thing would be that people claimed that the so-called bird broke into their house and made them study their French or any other language. Is a bird ruining the languages, or is it just a funny joke? Honestly no one knows!

Duolingo is a very good app considering the way it makes learning something hard seem fun. The app delivers all sorts of questions to you with little characters reacting to how you got an answer right or wrong. Duolingo is an app which is free, helps you learn, and teaches you to be punctual while doing anything. Now, a lot of us say we'll do something and then end up not doing it. Simple synonym of procrastination and while this is happening, Duolingo steps in with somewhat creepy messages to get you into doing something out of fear.

Overall, Duolingo is a great app which I hope you use. Just be thankful that you don't have Duolingo for your to-do list as well.

30
Stereotypes

Women are supposed to stay at home, wash dishes and mop up. Girls cannot go to school because their only job is to cook and look after the kids. This is a stereotypical issue that has been going on for centuries.

People assume that men and boys are to only be doing things like going to school, getting a job, voting, and if a man cooks or cleans then they are not behaving like a man. Whilst women only have three jobs. Cook, clean and look after the infants.

I'm not saying that she only has to do three things. I'm saying it because she can't do anything else without getting criticized. Simple words like, "she has no place in a school," or "of course she is emotional, she's a girl," and "what's the point in trying? Girls are never good at Math" are all stereotypical.

Mostly everyone still assumes that the mother cooks all the meals. Well, that is partly correct. I never said that it wasn't, just that her cooking isn't much appreciated.

Stereotypes

Now I'm going to be talking about boys. Boys are assumed to be in control, they shouldn't cook or clean, they should go to school, they shouldn't have long hair, and they cannot become a nurse, they can only become a doctor. These are very old stereotypes, but these are true. Lots of people don't judge boys and let them do what they want. But still there are lots of people who still don't approve of boys doing girl's work.

Now, there only so much a boy or a girl can do. Even more stereotypical, girls are often mimicked for wearing pink or doing anything that classifies them as a girl. For instance, someone would associate the word lipstick with a girl. Just because a girl uses lipstick doesn't mean only girls should. And from a boy's perspective, just because they play with footballs, doesn't mean that girls can't.

Gender stereotypes are causing more problems in this world. My only hope is that we learn to stop, and stereotypes won't change, unless we do.

31

Some movie suggestions for kids

Ever wanted to watch a movie, but never really had the chance? Well, fear not! I'm here to help you decide what movie to watch, and I bet by reading and watching these movies, you'll have tons of fun. Let the movie naming commence, here are some suggestions...

- SMCA (Secret Magic Control Agency) – The style of this movie is animation, the plot is about a king who rules a kingdom (the name wasn't given, I'm not sure) where magic and sorcery are forbidden without a license. An evil witch kidnaps the king. In this kingdom, if someone marries the king, they have the next level of magic. Two secret agents are on their way to save the king, but something happened on their way that impacted their entire search. I hope you watch this movie as it's fun and I love the story lines. It's quite funny!
- Matilda – We have all seen the old Matilda movie from Netflix, but the new and improved movie is

even better. Even though we all know the story line, who says we can't watch it again? Matilda is unfortunately brought up in a household which doesn't appreciate her talent. Even worse, her school principal is a big old meanie. So, what's Matilda gonna do about it? Watch and find out! The new movie, Matilda, is a musical, so be sure to check their wonderful musical numbers.

- Annie – This movie is about a girl who lives in a very secluded orphanage. The orphanage leader, Ms. Hannigan is very strict, and ends up drinking a lot, saying its medicine. Annie escapes, and then ends up living at a very famous person's house. But when problems start coming up and Ms. Hannigan is pulling out all the stops to get Annie back into the horrendous orphanage, what can Annie do to stop Ms. Hannigan and save the other girls? Watch it to find out!

Now the reason I picked out these three movies are because of their storyline and plot. These movies not only have very good morals and lessons, but the stories are also appropriate for children, and it has twist in story plots that will guarantee you pleasure. I hope you have a good time watching.

32
How to be the best person on earth

Everyone has their own opinions about how they can become better and change for better in what ways. Well, luckily for me, I know some about that type of information. Let me fill up your brain space with ideas.

Respect yourselves. Every great person respects themselves, and that begins with seeing yourself for you who you truly are, meaning peeling of any make up, tearing apart walls of self-criticism. Pretend you are being reborn, and you are seeing yourself for the first time. The next step to self-respect is to figure out your talents. Forget about your flaws, embrace those imperfections which make you, you.

Keep a clean bedroom. The most inventive masterminds had a clean room. Arrange your stuff in a way that is organised, and don't have any items across the room. This helps with discipline as well as keeping your room tidy. Keep your clothes of the floor, as well as regularly lighting a candle in your room. I would say once a week, or daily.

It really depends how much you want your room to smell good, but I suggest daily, for about an hour. That would be about a good enough time to read a book, which brings us to our next topic.

Read a LOT. Books not only feed us information, but they also help giving new words to use. Language is also a very tough barrier to break through, that's why reading is so important. It also helps our grammar, which is crucial in a lot of ways.

Getting to our point, being the best person on earth doesn't only mean being good at studies, it means being good at kindness as well. We need to be pure if we can succeed. So, with this information, I hope you have resolutions to become the best person you possibly can.

33

The struggles of being the elder and younger sibling

Most of us have siblings. If you don't then I'm not sure that you'll understand this one. But I will continue, regardless of somethings which don't make sense. Just a warning, some people may get affected by the outcome or what I say. Let's start with the younger sibling first.

The thoughts of a younger sibling are they enjoy being the youngest, because of the reason if they ever get hurt, they can roll around on the floor and create an excuse to get the older sibling in trouble. Those are the joys of being a younger sibling. Now, we will look into the struggles. The struggles of being a younger sibling is that sometimes you don't get all the attention. If you have a sibling which is a teen, you won't get much attention. You must also get bullied a lot, so you must have a buffalo skin. Now moving on to the elder sibling.

As the elder sibling, you get to tease and joke about your younger sibling, and being the eldest has its perks. Being in charge when mom and dad go out is a pretty good perk if I do say so myself. But the cons outweigh the pros itself. You get into a lot of trouble, as well as getting blamed for everything. When you have a rough day, those younger siblings just don't seem to understand and annoy you. When you finally get your room looking good, your younger sibling just come and jump on your bed.

So, hopefully from this topic you can understand how much siblings go through with each other. But what you need to take away from this topic is resilience. Siblings stick together no matter what happens, they are there together from beginning to the end. Even though siblings get into massive fights, they know they that they'll be fine. Siblingship is most important in every family. That's why we have family in the first place.

34
The three Rs.

We all know the three R's. Reduce, Reuse and Recycle. These are being taught in schools all over the world. These tell us how to be earth-friendly. There are also another set of three R's. Respect, Reconnect and Restore. Now, what really is the difference? Let's start with the first set.

Reduce, Reuse and Recycle. These specific R's are there to teach us how to be earth-friendly. Let's take the first one. Reduce. We must reduce the amount of plastic water bottles so that we can prevent more creatures from dying or going extinct in the ocean, as most plastic items take a few hundred years to fully recycle, and most are dumped into the ocean or wildlife. Reuse. Even if we do buy a plastic water bottle, we can use it again. Such as, buying and storing bags that are made from plastic, as we can use them again when we are going shopping, or simply filling up a plastic bottle and using it again. Recycle. Simply taking the effort to get rid of any unwanted items, mostly plastic.

Now to the second set. Respect. Respecting mother earth to make this earth a healthy and happy place.

We can show respect in many ways such as: planting trees, don't kick or throw stones at animals, and taking care of your garden. Reconnect. Reconnecting can be as simple as taking a walk in the park or taking a nature hike. Reconnecting can also mean more time offline than online, and spending time to enjoy all of nature. Restore. This one is more serious. We need to be alert. Animals such as tigers and pandas are coming closer to the extinction line than we thought they would. We need to restore the earth and help it. Because we are building more and more cities, animals are forced to leave their homes, wandering in the wrong climates in search of a home. We have left them with nothing as we take away their resources as well. Poaching is another problem which is leading animals to extinction. Restore doesn't mean just one thing. It means doing everything we can to save the animals as well as the earth, no matter. With some small actions, we can save the animals, the mother earth and we can save us.

35

How I love libraries and hate them at the same time

I LOVE TO READ. For that reason, I love to go to libraries and like to hang out with the reading community. Books are food to me. I like to devour them and spend hours eating and devouring them. But, as one human on this planet might ask, "then why do you hate the library?" Well, I am here to give ye thy information. Let us start with why I like the library.

I love the library because the community is always so friendly, and the books are so good. Also, the library always lets you to take books home for free, and wait for it… you have to bring them back. Now, another reason I'm obsessed is because libraries are places of peace and quiet. If you bring in a book, you will just simply find a seat and sit down there. The quietness brings us peace, as we would like to enjoy our books in silence. Another reason why I like libraries is because you have a variety of books, from all over the world. You could say that libraries are like international thrill ride. For all these reasons, I love libraries a lot. But, then why do I say I hate them? Well...

I love reading books, but in the flesh. If I'm reading something that's online, I lose interest quickly, as I want to feel the book. But libraries just make me greedy. It's funny how if I borrow a really good book, then I just must get it for myself. The thought of someone else reading my precious, perfect, awesome story just rips me apart. So, really, I want the books to myself to enjoy.

I love books and encourage others to get into the habit of reading as it can help us in a lot of ways. Reading is important, as much as living and breathing is!

www.ingramcontent.com/pod-product-compliance
Lightning Source LLC
LaVergne TN
LVHW021201160826
845679LV00024B/2194
* 9 7 9 8 8 9 2 3 3 7 5 9 5 *